ARTSCAPES

ARTSCAPES

Handwritten inscription:

For Bob Jangstaff —
Thanks for your interest!
See 71–73 to google the
Partworks. I look
forward to being
on your show)
Best,
lee 2/25/22

POEMS BY

LEE WOODMAN

SHANTI ARTS PUBLISHING
BRUNSWICK, MAINE

ARTSCAPES

Published by Shanti Arts Publishing
Interior and cover design by Shanti Arts Designs

Cover image: Craig Kraft, *Ancient Spiral
Symbol*, 2018. Neon on canvas. 25 x 22.5
x 2 inches. Used with permission.

Shanti Arts LLC
193 Hillside Road
Brunswick, Maine 04011
shantiarts.com

Printed in the United States of America

ISBN: 978-1-956056-12-9 (softcover)
ISBN: 978-1-956056-13-6 (ebook)

Library of Congress Control Number: 2021950332

for Susan Clampitt and Jeremy Waletzky

OTHER TITLES BY LEE WOODMAN

Homescapes (Finishing Line Press, 2020)

Mindscapes (Poets' Choice Publishing, 2020)

Lifescapes (Kelsay Books, 2021)

ARTIST'S STATEMENT

Often, I don't choose a work of art. It chooses me. From childhood I have been fascinated with artworks and evocative language. I find it strange but thrilling when a sculpture beckons, a painting demands I pay attention, or a piece of music asks: "You know what I'm talking about?" Through poetry, I can invite readers to walk into paintings, time travel through sculpture, and eavesdrop on conversations I have with artists. Enter a roaring boxing ring in Washington D.C., scramble into forty-thousand-year-old cave paintings in Indonesia, picture yourself in a harem's den in Algiers. A bronze globe, an avalanche, a Greek god— all provide image and metaphor for considering what it means to be mortal. They shed light on fears and fantasies, opening up views of an inexplicable world as only poetry can.

CONTENTS

ACKNOWLEDGMENTS 13

MARK ROTHKO, I CHALLENGE YOUR CLAIM 17
   —after Mark Rothko's *Untitled*, 1955

SELF-PORTRAIT, JASPER JOHNS 18
   —after Jasper Johns's *Field Painting*, 1963–64

VANQUOR 20
   —after Andy Warhol's *Mao*, 1973

A LIFE UNRAVELS WITH THE DAY 22
   —after Chelsea Welsh's *Caught in the Days Unraveling*, 2011–13

YVES BLUE 24
   —after Yves Klein's *Untitled Blue Sponge Relief*, 1960

WHO'S WATCHING WHOM? 26
   —after Henri Julien Rousseau's *The Equatorial Jungle*, 1909

TOO YOUNG TO UNDERSTAND 27
   —after Joan Miró's *Lunar Bird*, 1966–67

BOXING RING 28
   —after Mark Rothko's *Green and Maroon*, 1953

MEDUSA RETHINKS HER OWN DEATH 29
   —after Vanessa Zhao's *Head above Water*, 2019

SPIKY HAIRED WOMAN AT LEANG JING, SULAWESI, INDONESIA 30
   —after Craig Kraft's *Spiky Haired Woman*, 2017

A FATHER/DAUGHTER TALE 32
   —after Helen Zughaib's *Saying Goodbye*, 2018

STORY TOWER 34
   —inspired by Nikolai Rimsky-Korsakov's *Scheherazade*

GLOBE 36
   —after Arnaldo Pomodoro's *Sphere VI*, 1966

IN WHICH I CONSIDER MYSELF A POSSIBLE WOMAN OF ALGIERS ... 37
   —after Eugene Delacroix's *Women of Algiers in Their Apartment*, 1834

THE UNDERSIDE OF COLOR 40
   —after Marc Chagall's *Paris through the Window*, 1913

STAND UNDER A WILLOW 42
   —inspired by Stevie Wonder's "Superstition"

LITTLE SPIDER TRIPTYCH 44
   —after Alexander Calder's *Little Spider*, 1940

VOICES IN THE VOID 46
   —after Alberto Giacometti's *City Square*, 1948–49

BETWEEN STATES 48
   —after Joan Danziger's *Into the Magic*, 2007

AM I EITHER/OR 50
   —after Rupert Bunny's *Poseidon and Amphitrite*, c.1913

THREE ONSLAUGHTS 51
   —after Tacita Dean's *The Montafon Letter*, 2017

CONUNDRUM 55
   —after Henri Matisse's *Dance*, 1909

SOMETHING SEEMS FAMILIAR 56
   —after Gabrielle Widjaja's *Dance*, 2020

WHAT WE CARRY ON OUR BACKS 57
   —after Agnieszka Nienartowicz's *The Garden of Earthly Delights*, 2017

READING BOSCH BACKWARDS 60
   —after Hieronymus Bosch's *Garden of Earthly Delights*, 1490–1510

BLUE BOYS 62
   —after Thomas Ruff's *Self-Portrait*, 1991

PERENNIALS 64
   —after Salvador Dali's *Woman of Time*, 1973, cast 1984

THEY, ALIEN 66
   —after Huma Bhabha's *We Come in Peace*, 2018

PIAF SINGS LAVENDER 67
   —after Joan Mitchell's *La Vie en Rose*, 1979

A KIND OF GOSPEL 68
   —inspired by Leonard Cohen's "Hallelujah"

ART AND ARTISTS 71

THANKS 75

ABOUT THE AUTHOR 77

ACKNOWLEDGMENTS

My great appreciation to Lorette C. Luzajic, founding editor of *The Ekphrastic Review,* for publishing:

"Mark Rothko, I Challenge Your Claim"
"Self-Portrait, Jasper Johns"
"The Underside of Color"
"They, Alien"
"Who's Watching Whom"

To Annemarie Lockhart, founding editor, and Nathan Gunter, managing editor of *vox poetica,* for publishing:

"Vanquor"

To Montgomery College for publishing my poem in the exhibition *The Urge to Mark: Craig Kraft*:

"Spiky Haired Woman at Leang Jing, Sulawesi, Indonesia"

To Shanna McNair, founding editor and publisher, and Scott Wolven, consulting editor of *The New Guard,* for publishing:

"Voices in the Void"

To Donna Baier Stein, founder, and Lisa Sawyer, managing editor of *Tiferet Journal,* for publishing:

"Story Tower"

ARTSCAPES

Mark Rothko, I Challenge Your Claim

—after Mark Rothko's *Untitled*, 1955

Painting after painting after painting
hang like prayer flags.

A roomful of honor—
Tower, East side, National Gallery—

circular reading room with a single
pew from which to pay respects.

I ask you, "Why 'Untitled'?"
Would you not name a friend or

a child born, 1955? Here's what I see:
ochre-brown, black mouth screaming.

The shout so loud, it blurs the lips,
a forehead turns dark red in fury.

A weaker chin, pale white beneath,
move closer in, a pink stain shows.

I call you Anger On Top. Whispers
and vapors from steam rising upward,

I call you Tremble, Black Mouth,
teeth hidden behind the howl,

I call you White Question, hiding a hint
of fright below—you say "Untitled"—

Unbridled rage, suppressed dread,
I name it "This Time the Beast Wins."

SELF-PORTRAIT, JASPER JOHNS

—after Jasper Johns's *Field Painting*, 1963–64

"No pictures!" the guard at the gallery said,
"Not these three . . . "

All Jasper Johns. When asked "Why?"
he shrugged,

"Copyright issues I guess," or, "You know . . .
artists."

The conspicuous bright neon "R" got me,
and the mirror image of

carved letters down the middle—
a rectangular canvas split in two—

"Red, Yellow, Blue." Stenciled words,
theatrical lighting,

vivid color splotches on the left,
subdued hues on the right.

Savarin tin, Ballantine beer can, both
affixed, typical Pop—

familiar items from daily life,
tools he used in his workshop.

Jasper invites us to act, "Turn me
on, turn me off."

Flick the switch, the letters stand up,
lie down—akin to people.

The cityscape blinks on, blinks off,
Johns stays dark, referential.

He teases, he taunts, revealing small bits—
brush marks divulge, crosshatches hint.

However, no face. I hear his tacit plea,
"Please don't understand me too quickly."

VANQUOR

—after Andy Warhol's *Mao*, 1973

Mao chooses me
Massive man, square head, solid stance

Leader, CCP
Deep purple background, violet wash

I must stop
Struck still in the gallery, I conjure his maker,

Andy Warhol,
Because he's there too, golden plumage

Same two tufts,
Both heads the shape of Hello Kitty

Lurking from behind,
Warhol slips into the Chairman's left sleeve

Bodies morph,
Merge as portrait, breathe in unison

By reflex
My hand clasps my chest, autonomic gasp

I realize
They're wearing my blouse! Single button.

Three as one
We pledge allegiance, hands crossing hearts

Their countenance
Exactly mine—stony stare, contemplating—

Six nostrils
Blend into two, our lipstick is lavender

Our chins set,
Who is who? I am Chairman Mao

A Life Unravels with the Day

—after Chelsea Welsh's *Caught in the Days Unraveling*, 2011–13

A paisley wrap
thrown on a chair,
a burdened hairbrush
cast off there.

Auburn tresses
drown the bristles,
a dolphin rides
the purple handle.

Fair cousin Claire,
her hair grows thin,
she pulls the clumps,
as shedding begins.

Her boudoir somber,
door ajar,
a playful household
now macabre.

The cat slinks past,
the shades part-drawn,
a mirror hanging,
upholstery worn.

Shadows echo,
pots tip over,
rugs at angles,
orange, ochre.

Paint drips downward,
birds crouch low,
vines cascading,
shutters groan.

A barren life
her scalp will know,
when all is lost,
the cancer slow.

YVES BLUE

—after Yves Klein's *Untitled Blue Sponge Relief*, 1960

Surrender to the mystery,

experience the relentless hue—

let your limbs go limp.

Bathe in abstract obsession

of Blue Revolution—

succumb to the Klein void.

The voices of his sponges

cry vertiginous blue.

Sheer monochromes of

aerated pumice, haute-relief,

turn away from

oppressive steel-gray,

refuse the foul-brown of earth.

Impossible to make his color

behave, don't even try.

Float in the pocket of his sea,

wade in magic waters,

lift the arch of your foot.

Yield, or the enormity

will inseminate, impregnate,

crush you like a macaroon,

roll you like an airless puck.

Weighted bubbles of blue can

fall to the base of the canvas,

might fly vertical or horizontal.

Loaded pigment does not leak,

Utopia of unruly blue!

Yves's Ultramarine.

WHO'S WATCHING WHOM?

—after Henri Julien Rousseau's *The Equatorial Jungle*, 1909

Someone tried to rub out the moon,
light blurs in self-defense,
forest colors dim to blue-green camouflage.

Broad arms of leaves arch over the proscenium—
elbows of spades, bladed sprays of ferns.

Two creatures, center-stage, stare.
Furry mute father, owl or bearded man.
Raccoon or gorilla son, X-nose, flashlight eyes,
ears on high alert.

Hyacinth of wisdom stands sentry on the right,
directs the pointed stage lights below
to keep guard, hold fire, maintain calm.

Henri Julien retells this play,
jungle upon jungle—Madagascar,
New Caledonia, Brazil, Peru,
Macedonia, Mexico.

Scenes repeat scenes, forests of mystery,
the hidden scout! Rousseau's voyeur
perched on a bent branch,
high over cuckoo-flowers—
a man-bird, small-beaked, shrouded by
ill-fitting trench coat and cape,
witnesses all. Who knows?

Hours pass, sky smudges away,
a lion passes by, tail swinging.
Rousseau recedes in the wings,
a perfect stage manager.

TOO YOUNG TO UNDERSTAND

—after Joan Miró's *Lunar Bird*, 1966–67

Years ago, I went to see the Lunar Bird
    A god in prized museum space
    Part bull, part bird
    Aqueduct legs firmly grounded
    Unicorn nose pointing upwards
    He exuded insight
    Guarded secrets I wanted

Compelled to go again
    To pay my votive offering
    Alas, he stood alone
    Deported to a garden
    Pale gray grasses blew, all weeds
    His cupped wings flailing
    Disdainful, I hurried past the past

Now doomed terrestrial
    He is dumbed
    No longer hears celestial voices
    A disappearing sun
    Won't warm his shoulders
    Mournful tunes rise and die
    Chants disappear into silence

Finally, I come in shame
    Quietly my Lunar Bird tells me
    He's condemned to storage
    Weakened in isolation
    Bronze shoulders worn by touches
    Messages lost in his lungs
    My former praise only noise in wind

BOXING RING

—after Mark Rothko's *Green and Maroon*, 1953

Sitting in the Rothko Room—all walls, no windows—
alone, staring at
green upon maroon, framed by windowsill blue

I'm pulled, pulled into that green patch
blinking, and there a
white ghost returns repeatedly, oscillating

Invisible crowds roar around us, cheering
for the bully
They are believers, for them, this is a true match

The gauzy white champ is dizzy,
reeling from swollen
black mitts that keep arcing around

Shouters press toward the maroon platform,
edging toward
beige bristled ropes that divide us

All quiet now, I block out clatter
Green blurs over and flurries
The white ghost never retreats to a corner

With quickening clarity, the stage flattens out
Carmine-maroon rectangle remains
Firm blue frame holds it all together

A drip of white blood leaks from the frame

MEDUSA RETHINKS HER OWN DEATH

—after Vanessa Zhao's *Head above Water*, 2019

Terror sleeps with me at night, creeps behind my eyes
Which open in fear with giant irises

Feverish migraines clamp my forehead
Moans of weakness, I can't turn over

Limp legs no longer carry me, my kidneys shrivel
In rancid urine, virus clings like sharp pins

To the white scars of my lungs
A machine rattle signals I'm ready to die

I bow to nurse, Perseus, who covers my body
He removes my head, my serpentine hair

Gently he lays me on the surface of an icy stream
Spreads my locks like a ganglia of lapis

I have been saved, sclerotized in white porcelain
Now I am an amulet

My tears are fixed pebbles of azurite, semi-precious
Red rivulets of veins will fade in time

My Buddha gaze no longer kills, solid and serene
Strong protection for the hopeful

I bow to all who carry me, a clay coin in your pocket
A stamped rosary bead on your string

SPIKY HAIRED WOMAN AT LEANG JING, SULAWESI, INDONESIA

—after Craig Kraft's *Spiky Haired Woman*, 2017

She holds dominion
from an ancient cave.
By flickering candlelight,
her rust oxide profile emerges—
slender shoulders, sturdy head.
Partially hidden
by lichen and algae,
the timeworn markings ring
with intention.
Resolute woman,
her lips protrude,
her hair a headdress,
cascade of wiry strands.
She lassos a small beast.
The neon artist captures
the Woman, borrows her
forty-thousand-year-old
image. He burns her
life into the present,
makes her glow holy,
brick-red neon.
Her voice indelible,
she sends strong messages:
Good hunting here.
Beware of rivals.
Animals die out.
Vicious volcano.
Drawings erode, yet
Spiky Haired Woman
lifts the veil
for the sculptor
to spirits beyond.

He follows a
sacred tradition—
Making new marks,
he leaves his light.

A FATHER/DAUGHTER TALE

—after Helen Zughaib's *Saying Goodbye*, 2018

Exuberant, joyful colors—her painting beckons—
Golden sky of sand and promise
Distant rolling hills of jade
Royal blue waves unravel the tale

Aunts and cousins gather to wave good-bye
Three travelers, feet firmly grounded
On familiar earth,
Stare back at their homeland, 1946

Ma'a salaam, ma'a salaam, all melt from yearning,
Ma'a salaam, ma'a salaam

They prepare to leave, trunks marked "Libnan"
Mother clutches passports in a tube,
Elia, grasps a rug from Dimashq
Relatives who stay behind face the sea

Who and what is family?
Where and what is home to separated kin?
White roosters strut between them,
Marking the dividing line

Ma'a salaam, ma'a salaam, the rowboat arrives. Hurry!
Ma'a salaam, ma'a salaam

One last view—mountain village, orange roof tiles,
Rural scene they all knew, the smell of cedar,
Aunt Salwa's white mandeel,
A silent steed bears witness

The child who held the rug is now the father
Who tells family stories in cautious words
She who holds the brush paints patterns,
Strokes in technicolor bid we listen,

Demand we hear the sounds
After all the truth may lie not in the speaking
But in the images of silence

Ma'a salaam, Ma'a salaam, Ma'a salaam

STORY TOWER

—inspired by Nikolai Rimsky-Korsakov's *Scheherazade*

Building story on story
Balcony by balcony
Windows with blinds—

        We frame our lives

Four oboes take us forward,
We heed recurring themes
A river flows unwinding

        with currents underneath

The leavings too familiar,
Arpeggios gone rogue
Each day a chapter lengthens,

        each year the epic grows

We deflect, we hide in labor,
Five trumpets push us on
We raise the shades of mourning,

        a seed becomes a rose

We soften as two harps wrap
Around the violins
Torment melts to forgiveness,

        reprise becomes reprieve

There's a rhythm to our days now,
Remorse and anguish end
We know this lilting story

      we climb the stairs again

We need one thousand stories,
To fall in love so slowly
A tender piccolo's refrain—

      standing on balconies,
      I remain

GLOBE

—after Arnaldo Pomodoro's *Sphere VI*, 1963–65

A crumpled earth at knee level
tilts in the Hirshhorn Sculpture garden—

an aching face, gaping crevasses,
a forced cracked smile.

Once astronauts marveled,
now the Blue Planet is ravaged—
rusted to dirty brown, hardened.

So like the Coliseum in Rome,
when first built, beatific—
perfect concentrics with arches
covered in marble—
before men gouged out lives,
plunged swords into
golden lions' flesh.

Sphere 6 of solid shining
bronze, perhaps mimicking
a globe of shining oceans
once unscarred—
now reveals jagged craters.
Without pretense, shows
underlying pock marks,
scarred metal, angry iron teeth.

All bring to mind interior
traps, forced grimaces,
stifled worlds. A sculpture,
cast in time, still screams
into the future.

In Which I Consider Myself a Possible Woman of Algiers

—after Eugene Delacroix's *Women of Algiers in Their Apartment*, 1834

Delacroix, like me, is charmed but deluded,
fascinated by their harem allure—
luscious flesh, bejeweled bodices,
vibrant costumes, figs.

Entering through swinging saloon doors,
I pose for them.
My magenta bloomers are brighter than theirs,
my cheeks burn violet energy.

They do not look my way,
I am disturbing the languor, familiar stupor.
Leaning on thick rugs, bolstered pillows,
these plump doyennes are adorned

with gold necklaces that sparkle against
nude chests, coyly covered by see-
through muslin blouses.
Turkish turned-up sandals,

thrown to the side, reveal
meaty feet, pudgy toes.
At times, our ladies shift positions
to ease a hip or elbow—discomfort

does not suit them.
Bored with the hookah,
they compare the men
they bedded last night:

a corpulent prince with lacquered hair;
sanctimonious merchant, smelling of musk;
odoriferous suitor, stale wine, spunk.

Spiritless, they wait uncounted hours,
tomorrow night will be a repeat.
Blue-black Algerian servant,
Samia, turns away from them,
she's heard it all before.
The mirror on the tiled wall above them
tilts forward, she has not bothered
to straighten it.

She stops abruptly when she sees me.
Am I a new consort?
She determines not,
we are kindred spirits she and I,

different kinds of gems.
We recognize this luxuriant space as dark,
light shines through a depressed window
but to no end.

It doesn't go anywhere,
only opens to the kitchen
where Samia is headed.
I believe it leads to Exodus—

We could run fast,
holding hands to escape this confinement.
As I attempt to find my way
across the circle of ladies,
a putrid smell rises—

moths in the drapes, cockroaches
in the corner, truth exhaling
from the rotten flesh of women
under those bloomers.

Dressed-up dolls dulled by men
who tell them they are well-taken care of
don't realize their pearl anklets,
endless hashish, servants-in-waiting keep them

captive for life.
I pick my way through an airless world
across plush carpets to follow brave Samia.

At least, Delacroix had foresight to render her
with fleet feet and shoes on.

THE UNDERSIDE OF COLOR

—after Marc Chagall's *Paris through the Window*, 1913

Chagall invites me to his house—he knows I love this painting.

He leaves the front door open, I arrive early.
Seated on the right side of the parlor,
locket in my palm, I wait.

Chenille, nervous cat, emerald green tail, sits on the sill listening.
Shouts from the street are loud, one side of the window is open.

Aromatic warm baguettes, clinking cups from the café below.
Colors roar across the sky—

swaths of vermilion, streaks of royal blue, icy white shafts
illuminate the sky turning the Eiffel Tower shimmering white.

The spire shares light with rows of dollhouse-size dwellings
and wraps a beam around the right side of my head.

Et voilà! We're startled by the oncoming whoosh
of Chagall's parachute rushing toward us,
plummeting down toward his floral-back chair.
He lands, offers absinthe—

he's happy, he's sad. He had a vision of his parents descending—
miniature black horizontal figures floating head to head,
bickering in joyful Yiddish.

They stay with him everywhere, wave as he passes.
They know how he loves Paris, beautiful Bella,
why he paints his fish, fancy fiddlers, harlequin clowns.

Behind buoyant colors, someone is saying Kaddish.
Sadness seeps from the city smoke stacks.
We sip, melding into lament.

Chenille jumps down, slinks to the kitchen, sniffing for herring.
She knows Chagall adores her,
comes back to rub her neck up his trouser leg.

He's laughing, he's sobbing.
Fantasy and gravity counter-balance.
My two heads, two hearts weep with love and contradiction.

STAND UNDER A WILLOW

—inspired by Stevie Wonder's "Superstition"

Stand under a willow
Protect yourself from harm
Stand under a willow
Breathe in scented balm

Canopy to shade you
Branches green and strong
Graceful boughs to shield you
Banish all that's wrong

Nightmares cannot kill you
Pain will dissipate
Bend into the tempest
Wave bad ghosts away

Willow sways with wind-song
Soothing as a lyre
Harbinger of sweet spring
Always first to flower

Tune in sounds of insects
Worries disappear
Trust the tree will linger
Long roots absorb fear

Some have sipped the nectar
To make a healing brew
Learn from their traditions
Change your point of view

Birds line nests with catkins
Hatchlings rest at ease
Follow on their secrets
Lie down, feel the breeze

Stay under the willow
Believe in sacred signs
Fantasies you long for
Will come true in time

Willows near the river
Reflections holding hands
They have understandings
They don't understand

LITTLE SPIDER TRIPTYCH

—after Alexander Calder's *Little Spider*, 1940

1
Spider prepares his performance,
splays and pliés for take-off,

twists and dangles a spray of
long and longer legs.

Maybe exploring a garage wall,
a dark corner to crouch,

could be displaying his plumage—
red, black, yellow.

Alone in his venture,
he hangs pendulously,

dropping several bulbous eyes
behind pedipalp pincers.

Avenger or retreater,
his venom not enough to kill,

he shakes, flutters when disturbed—
a dancing blur of frenzy.

What will stay with me:
the grace of the whirl coming

to rest, a stabile perched on air.

2
I swear it grew in the museum overnight,
taller, more agile, more spidery.

Queen Arachnid now, on her perch
among the Calder Creatures, plotting . . .

This time not just sheet metal,
paint, and wire . . . but a She Spider,

tense as a spring ready to uncoil.
Her organs droop with heavy birth,
displaying a line-up to her heart

She stalks now, not crouching,
confidence towering, eye cocked up.

3
Cantilevered by black sac,
Little Spider has spine, fierce stability.

Did Alexander care if he/she/they
were a spider or Arachnid,

Daddy-Long-Legs, or even a-live?
This could be merely a balancing act—

a web of counter-balance,
perhaps a rhythmic gesture.

What stays with me now:
A visitor asks her friend—

graceful androgyne, a pregnant dancer—

"What do you call that?
I don't think it's really a sculpture."

VOICES IN THE VOID

—after Alberto Giacometti's *City Square*, 1948–49

Alberto,
You are far from us now,
though 1966 is not so long gone.
Pericardial fluid hardened around your heart,
locking it in cement. You left sculptures of all kinds—
miniature cast models trapped in matchboxes,
giant plodding statues, skeletal dogs lurking.
I follow one set of shadows
across a lonely plaza, City Square.
Five figures pose a fleeting sight as they move
through a gigantic expanse of nothingness.
Blade-thin silhouettes—misshapen heads,
huge hollow eyes,
chins thrust out, Adam's Apples sinking.
Four of the five attempt to stride in different directions
across the deserted pavement, but their ponderous feet
strain upward at the heel,
never escaping the merciless hold of the slab.
One does not even try.
She is static, sclerotic—extracted, pinched, striated,
gouged, charred.

I call to her, "Ava?"
Loud and bold, the males chant first:

"We are tensile, strong as iron,
with captured feet of clay.
Our someplace badly bombed and burned,
all that's left is sex and death.
We hang to our intensity,
we thrust our knife heads forward.
We cannot look at women,
in them we feel our shame."

At last, sound courses upward
through constricted vocal cords
and lodges behind her eye sockets.
Through those wide holes, a choking solo:

"I want them to touch my
golden curls frozen in bronze—
to understand that one breast
droops in memory,
to know how my arms are battened to
my sides, how my hands, clumps of
stone, hide against my knees.
This hardened lump of genitals
has fused between my hips.
Touch me. Lift me."

The square falls silent.

With respect and concern,
I plead for these exiles wrapped in emptiness:
"Are they choking or chanting,
falling forever, or rising with hope?
In this city void, they walk as ghosts,
as spirits met in dreams.
They make the action vanish,
they make the present vanish.
Why did you chip them all away,
peel and leave them as husks?
No accordions fill the City Square,
no giddy partners dance on cobblestones.
You have not sculpted human figures,
just shadows of castaways.
In the name of God, and Ava, of
humanity, and flesh,
Release them!"

BETWEEN STATES

—after Joan Danziger's *Into the Magic*, 2007

In this year of metamorphosis
of divorce, of COVID-19,
of transplanting to a place where I know no one,

I re-discover "Into the Magic," a forest world,
table-top scale: horses fleeing,
phantasmagoric creatures prancing. Carnival and funeral.

The sorceress shapes her clay,
molding curved tree branches, open-palmed hands
with wiry fingers reaching heavenward.

Exposed roots pregnant with pith
protect a cast of little equestrians riding puppet horses.
Powerful spirits: some dash inward; others escape outward.

A demon horse and rider chase a riderless steed;
a whitish angel-figure, galloping,
prays for deliverance.

In this year of metamorphosis, the sculptor invites me
to make my own myth. I linger longer, pry deeper.
Fear and fantasy rub shoulders. I dream of a strange

ceremony, where I receive a yearbook
rather than a diploma. Each graduate has
a page of memories, pictures, sayings—mine is blank.

In this year of metamorphosis, I am between
happiness of habitat and treacherous terrain.
I wish for infrared night vision to distinguish

between wolves or sheep below,
to discern if stiff pink hyacinths offer poison or shade,
and whether this zone of ambiguity will lift.

I must fly like a bat into baby banyan trees,
shelter in woodpecker holes, celebrate
my homeless body hanging from a hopeful brain.

AM I EITHER/OR

—after Rupert Bunny's *Poseidon and Amphitrite*, c.1913

Am I horse, or am I man? I feel fury, darts can poison,
yet, while hidden with the lambs, woolly kindness wraps my hands

At first, I play with naked sirens, splashing up the friendly seas,
then I thrust them with my trident, man or woman, both I seize

I drown them all to depths below where gleaming palace lies
Sharp barbed coral tears their knees, opens fleshy thighs

Even so, I build new islands, shelter clans so they might live,
safeguard my beloved cities—in my heart, I yearn to give

My rage arises soon again, I do compete with gods and men
I hate to lose, one prize I covet, Athena knows it—and she wins

I free my horses—stamp, bite, trample, cut her cheek with iron rust,
I can rise above her city, I could quake the earth to dust

But I am so very weary, why unfurl these savage waves,
I would rather bathe with dolphins, pet the lambs, hold mermaids safe

THREE ONSLAUGHTS

—after Tacita Dean's *The Montafon Letter*, 2017

1

Scant seconds

for escape exist

when an avalanche

is triggered.

Heavy slabs of ice

slide past

weaker platforms.

Cliffs collapse,

snowfall slams

down the pathway

submerging victims,

who cup

their mouths,

trying to carve

air pockets to breathe.

A letter from Austria

tells of the Torrent

centuries ago—

Montafon, 1689.

Three hundred perished.

A village priest

climbed high

to bless the dead,

calm the living,

when he was buried by

a second seismic slide.

Suddenly,

a massive third

avalanche

uncovered him, alive.

2

Moved by this marvel,

Tacita Dean spray paints

the alpine scene,

liquid chalk

on a gigantic blackboard,

thunderous

clouds of snow landing

in giant white clumps

at the base. She writes

tiny phrases

on bare ledges,

her dedication

to the lost.

The artist speaks

"avalanche," but

not only of cliffs.

We mourn

the black backdrop,

the torrent of

white terror

triggered by a rogue

unearthing rocks,

destabilizing mountains.

We implore

a third downrush

to bring us

to our senses,

uncover our best selves.

CONUNDRUM

—after Henri Matisse's *Dance*, 1909

Light comes from behind illuminating a mural in motion—
five audacious nudes, straight black hair, float weightlessly
into emerald green, cerulean blue

Attached and unattached, bound in rhythms of relentless circles
Unclear as to who leads and who follows, it doesn't matter
One pushes, one reaches, others glance down

A painter no longer needs to be pre-occupied by details
Fling the color, hue the gesture, heed the orchestra
Toss tradition, liberate the farandole—it's just a sketch

Murmurs of Modigliani, shades of Stravinsky sneak in—
the music hastens, violins beat like frantic footsteps,
flutes blow elongated bodies into sinuous whirling

Like recurring dreams, strangers and places meld in the sixth sense
Earth or cloud, ocean or sky, family or stranger, who cares?
Worries infiltrate these unknown maidens, cast in a spell

Wait! It does matter, we must give ear. Bacchanalia, ode to joy,
mock abduction, or trance—these figures keep orbiting,
convinced they can save each other wrapped in dance.

SOMETHING SEEMS FAMILIAR

—after Gabrielle Widjaja's *Dance*, 2020

Henri Matisse's figures dance au naturel,
Widjaja takes the canon west to east.
Demoiselles, in colorful graphic, gracefully complete
the circle. Clasping hands, they pass tall groundswells.

Dressed in red Qipao, they perform a danse nouvelle,
and slyly reclaim heritage, profound and bittersweet.
Henri Matisse's figures dance au naturel,
Widjaja takes the canon west to east.

With humor, she calls her artworks "Gentle Oriental,"
eager to taste, infuse her kindred background—Chinese—
Sans apology, she appropriates with glee.
Her group of femmes fatales prance parallel,
standing on shoulders of those who danced au naturel.

We've seen this before.
Five women clutching hands dance near the shore.
Volcanoes erupt in the ocean nearby, with waves
swirling round propelled by the force.
But wait, the dancers are wearing traditional dress,
their hair up in buns, is this a painting? Or,
a print that is numbered, a stamp of Chinese?

I search for a form, and realize at once—
all art is wild capture, all life is pre-learned.
What we have read has been written before;
what we hear now are recomposed scores.
And yet, all re-imagined, so fresh and new,
astonishing remnants spurt masterful bloom.

What We Carry on our Backs

—after Agnieszka Nienartowicz's *The Garden of Earthly Delights*, 2017

Trompe l'oeil? It must be a tattoo,

covering the soft skin of a maiden's lower back,

flowing up past her angel wings,

around the nape of her neck,

wisps of blond hair trailing down

the side of an unseen face.

Others know what she carries, but

she cannot see this playground of corruption

that rides her—

Shameless nudes

riding horseback in the meadow,

voyeur birds, beaks extended,

peering at men's bodies,

legs akimbo in the lake,

hands on genitalia.

She carries the scene lightly

as if she donned a veiled leotard—

nonetheless, she is imbued

with enormous weight,

permanently inked.

The artist cast the original

mystery, Bosch's story from 1490,

dyeing it onto her model's pale skin.

Implications of human's fallen nature

persists through centuries,

tales of flesh figures

cavorting on canvas, cloth,

tee-shirts, posters, emojis on screen.

We gasp, blush, scrutinize the surface,

gulping for more:

    sin?

    debauchery?

    joy?

    delight?

A Higher Painter imagined it first,

a contrast within a contradiction—

pierced through all flesh,

sunken into souls,

sketched on our backs.

No one knows how long the pigment will last.

READING BOSCH BACKWARDS

—after Hieronymus Bosch's *Garden of Earthly Delights*, 1490–1510

The landscape is black, monstrous creatures lurk,
explosions set cities on fire, crowds flee, demons speed by
on icy lakes, skeletons climb gallows to reach rooftops in vain.

The "Tree-Man" crouches, body contorted like a dead oak,
a disc table on his head supporting a putrid pink bagpipe.

"Bird-King" sits on a chamber pot, eating corpses
and excreting them through a blue bubble into a cavern.

Disgust, fascination,
Hallucination?

I fly over a kaleidoscopic garden teeming with nudes
who mingle, play and tantalize. I puzzle over males and females,
clutching engorged strawberries and plums.

I meet flamboyant creatures, horned and beaked,
crawling and cavorting around the scene—spotted fish,
blue-balled boars, and urchins with fans of spears on their backs.

I trapeze through this lush playground of greenery,
where gymnasts perform headstands, crowds caress each other,
touch bottoms, offer cherries.

Alarmed, enticed, I scan the triptych backward—right to left—
choosing to refuse doom.

Confusion, disorientation,
Dream?

How sweet the white-spotted giraffe, the elephant lumbering
toward a unicorn among horses. A baby owl,
peering from a cave in the fountain, his curiosity palpable.

Oh, the wonder of soaring with birds through open arcs,
looping back to dive into color—to graze the bodies, savor the fruits.
Picking bliss of pure faith, freedom from original sin, I opt for Hope.

I bless the cloaked elder, pray he is there to enfold
the young woman's hand, and encourage the reclining man
to extend his feet, to brush the flowing robe.

BLUE BOYS

—after Thomas Ruff's *Self-Portrait*, 1991

Two images of a man within the same frame,
twin-like but not.

One notes:

I look like me,
but I stand differently in back.

Notice how I present, shoulders more crouched,
softer gaze, hair slightly kinkier

covering one eye, hand in front dangling eyeglasses,
pinky lifted. Some would say flexible, gregarious,
impulsive, a performance artist.

Except, I'm behind too,
more direct stare, broader nose and face,
a thin-lipped analyst, business man
with an attitude of surety, decisive.

All exist, like Faces of Eve:

Artist Thomas Ruff, captures a surface, prepared in studio—
dead-pan, unemotional, nonetheless, full of feeling.

His two blue boys, with rigor of self-surveillance,
insist on distinct personalities.
How would you know the full story?

One might have lost his passport,
anxious about identity theft. One could work as a designer
at Apple, be a broker, drive a truck. Dress codes defy.

A shrink once said to them,
"Don't show me photos of your family; they'll all be smiling."

PERENNIALS

—after Salvador Dali's *Woman of Time*, 1973, cast 1984

I, Gold Rose, prevail
And speak for us all—
Patina Lady, statuesque,
Your gold gown swirling,
Folds falling to your feet

Your right arm raised
Holds me high
Your left arm, bent
At the elbow, supports
Golden Time,
Melting in surrender

Old souls all,
We witness hours pass,
Day and night warp,
Seasons advance, we've
Known each other well

I will be the lighthouse,
Emit metal beams, send
Our distinct shadow
Outward to ensure earthly
Beings we will care for you

We will not drop you
We are eternal
Rose, unyielding
Lady, protecting
Time, soothing

Disparate objects,
Encased in bronze,
Strange plinthe-fellows,
We three stand firm
Merged in one by Dali.
Unflagging, we fold,
Bend, reach out to stars.
Dali invites
Us to remember our birth—
Soft lost wax of dreams

THEY, ALIEN

—after Huma Bhabha's *We Come in Peace*, 2018

They come in peace, standing stone still
outside a White House.
Tall—one might guess forged of clay,
cork and bronze, perhaps papier mâché—
one pink head, four faces in each direction,
black nostrils flaring, torso of turquoise,
massive chest with yellow nipple studs,
abdomen and legs that turn black below the belly
with forearms pressed against trousers
down to space boy boots.

You terrified them, you militia of horseback,
guards of gun men.
They bare themself to you with love,
red and yellow vagina bearing
witness, bulbous black penis
and scrotum to the left side.
The upturned eye lashes
on their voluminous breasts say they are open,
raise no arm to fight, no weapon to harm.
They are the Goddess of Everywhere.
Urdu tattoos in royal blue and orange
cover both arms, Jewish stars on one forehead,
Native American braids down the back,
an arrow toward two fleshy buttocks
marked with orange dots.
You see them as prehistoric or apocalyptic;
they come in peace.

Now, you killers are the Other.

PIAF SINGS LAVENDER

—after Joan Mitchell's *La Vie en Rose*, 1979

Music and landscape make me want to paint
And paint I did, four canvasses, side by side,
lilac-tinted panorama of love.
Wide swaths of lyrical lavender,
dipping into pink, gray, underscored by
black vertical chords beneath,
strumming intently toward consummation.

Across a crowded room
The first panel is my most intense,
the first surprise wail—infatuation mirrors
addiction; the orchestra plays on,
a sensuous saxophone pleads, there is no
shy sweetness here, his gaze anchors in my eyes;
I'm embarrassed by how unoriginal the scene.

Je vois la vie en rose
A world of lavender quiets to light pink
as I catch my breath. Drumbeats sink as I try
to remember all clichés: the memory of a palm
over my hand, a hesitant leaning in to kiss,
hands sliding past my waist to cup my hips;
obsession and compulsion are symbiotic.

He told me, swore it for life
Lavender returns in force, brushstrokes scattered,
more ecstatic, a body pushes forth, center stage.
Not-giving-a-damn, I fling myself in. My breast is full,
I may explode, covered with color.
Sometimes Eros walks softly, I know that love is close.
I sink.

A KIND OF GOSPEL

—inspired by Leonard Cohen's "Hallelujah"

the way Leonard sang it was highly religious
in a sexual way,
highly sexual in a religious way
k.d. Lang took it over the top
Hallelujah
Hallelujah

lyrics about tying someone in a chair,
cutting locks of hair, highly rousing,
highly rhythmic, orgasmic
Hallelujah

and now in our time of plague
more and more faces in sequestered places
come on line one by one, pleading
Hallelujah

how the golden screen heals
during Time of Terror
individuals once cold and broken,
a youth choir no more lost and groping

families link through distant chords
we sing the song one hundred times
exquisite faces in sequestered places
find our voices, reaching, stretching,
when we could not feel, we learned to touch

maybe there's a Soul above, we want,
we hope, we pray for love
a melancholic, fragile

Hallelujah, Hallelujah, Hallelujah, Hallelujah!

glory, glory, glory, glory—
guitar keeps walking baseline,
lone saxophone fades slowly,
an everlasting song always ends in silence

ART AND ARTISTS

[17] Mark Rothko, *Untitled*, 1955. Oil on canvas. 105 x 93 inches (266.7 x 236.2 cm). National Gallery of Art, Washington, D. C.

[18] Jasper Johns, *Field Painting*, 1963–64. Oil on canvas with objects. 72 x 36.7 inches (182.8 x 93.2 cm). Private collection.

[20] Andy Warhol, *Mao*, 1973. Acrylic and silkscreen on canvas. 50.1 x 42.3 inches (127.3 x 107.6 cm). National Gallery of Art, Washington, D. C.

[22] Chelsea Welsh, *Caught in the Days Unraveling*, 2011–13. Photograph.

[24] Yves Klein, *Untitled Blue Sponge Relief*, 1960. Pigment, natural sponges, and pebbles on board. 78 x 64.7 inches (199 x 165 cm). Glenstone, Potomac, Maryland.

[26] Henri Julien Rousseau, *The Equatorial Jungle*, 1909. Oil on canvas. 55.3 x 51 inches (140.6 x 129.5 cm). National Gallery of Art, Washington, D. C.

[27] Joan Miró, *Lunar Bird*, 1966–67. Bronze. 89.3 x 88.5 x 58.2 inches (207.0 x 204.9 x 147.8 cm). Hirshhorn Museum and Sculpture Garden, Washington, D. C.

[28] Mark Rothko, *Green and Maroon*, 1953. Oil on canvas. 91.1 x 54.8 inches (231.4 x 139.3 cm). The Phillips Collection, Washington, D. C.

[29] Vanessa Zhao, *Head above Water*, 2019. Polymer clay head with acrylic paints. 15.7 x 15.7 x 1.9 inches (40 x 40 x 5 cm).

[30] Craig Kraft, *Spiky Haired Woman*, 2017. Neon and wood. 28 x 36 x 4 inches (71.1 x 91.4 x 10.1 cm).

[32] Helen Zughaib, *Saying Goodbye* (from the series *Stories My Father Told Me*), 2018.

[34] Nikolai Rimsky-Korsakov, *Scheherazade*, 1888.

[36] Arnaldo Pomodoro, *Sphere VI*, 1963–65. Bronze. Hirshhorn Museum and Sculpture Garden, Washington, D. C.

[37] Eugene Delacroix, *Women of Algiers in their Apartment*, 1834. Oil on canvas. 70.8 x 90.1 inches (180 x 229 cm). Louvre Museum, Paris, France.

[40] Marc Chagall, *Paris through the Window*, 1913. Oil on canvas. 53.5 x 55.8 inches (136 x 141.9 cm). Guggenheim, New York City.

[42] Stevie Wonder, "Superstition," 1972.

[44] Alexander Calder, *Little Spider*, 1940. Painted sheet metal and wire. 43.7 x 50 x 55 inches (111.1 x 127 x 139.7 cm). National Gallery of Art, Washington, D. C.

[46] Alberto Giacometti, *City Square*, 1948–49. Bronze. 9.5 x 25.5 x 17.1 inches (24.0 x 64.7 x 43.4 cm). National Gallery of Art, Washington, D. C.

[48] Joan Danziger, *Into the Magic*, 2007. Mixed media. 34 x 45.2 x 32.5 inches (86.4 x 114.9 x 82.7 cm). Smithsonian American Art Museum, Washington, D. C.

[50] Rupert Bunny, *Poseidon and Amphitrite*, c.1913. Oil on canvas. 25.6 x 31.9 inches (65.2 x 81.2 cm). National Gallery of Australia, Canberra.

[51] Tacita Dean, *The Montafon Letter*, 2017. Chalk on blackboard. Nine panels, each 48 x 96 inches (122 x 244 cm). Glenstone, Potomac, Maryland.

[55] Henri Matisse, *Dance*, 1909. Oil on canvas. 102.5 x 153.5 inches (259.7 x 390.1 cm). Museum of Modern Art, New York City.

[56] Gabrielle Widjaja, *Dance*, 2020.

[57] Agnieszka Nienartowicz, *The Garden of Earthly Delights*, 2017. Oil on canvas. 35.4 x 23.6 inches (90 x 60 cm).

[60] Hieronymus Bosch, *Garden of Earthly Delights*, 1490–1510. Oil on canvas. 80.9 x 150 inches (205.5 x 384.9 cm). The Prado Museum, Madrid, Spain.

[62] Thomas Ruff, *Self-Portrait*, 1991. Chromogenic print. 73.1 x 71.1 x 1.5 inches (185.7 x 180.7 x 3.8 cm). National Gallery of Art, Washington, D. C.

[64] Salvador Dali, *Woman of Time*, 1973, cast 1984. Bronze. 25.6 x 6.7 inches (65 x 17 cm).

[66] Huma Bhabha, *We Come in Peace*, 2018. Bronze and paint. 152.5 x 48 x 43.6 inches (387.4 x 121.9 x 110.8 cm). Hirshhorn Museum and Sculpture Garden, Washington, D. C.

[67] Joan Mitchell, *La Vie en Rose*, 1979. Oil on canvas. 110.3 x 268.2 inches (280.3 x 681.3 cm). The Metropolitan Museum, New York City.

[68] Leonard Cohen, "Hallelujah," 1984.

THANKS

I am grateful to the people who made this book possible:

my sister and first reader, novelist Betsy Woodman, who keeps me laughing

my master poets, critics and publishers: Grace Cavalieri, the late Chris Bursk, Sue Ellen Thompson, Richard Blanco, Alexandra Oliver, Lorette Luzajic, Jane Rosenberg LaForge, Richard Harteis, Leah Maines, and Karen Kelsay

writers from the priceless Monday group, who kindly welcomed a poet among novelists: Elizabeth Berg, Mary Mitchell, Donna Stein, and Betsy Woodman

my writing companions and cherished friends: Bill Kircher, Stephanie Cotsirilos, Tanner Stening, Virginia Rice, Sarah Toth, Randy Wynn, Julianna Jacobson, Pete Chauvette, Susan Clampitt, and Jeremy Waletzky

the talented women who made reading and writing so healing during the pandemic and into the future: Dawn Raffel, Estelle Erasmus, Jill Smolove, Jane Rosenberg LaForge, Donna Stein, Betsy Woodman, Laura Weiss, Joanna Laufer, Ronna Weinberg, Pamela Walker, and Ellen Prentiss Campbell

the magical visionaries at The Writer's Hotel and *The New Guard: Literary Review:* founding editor, Shanna McNair, and consulting editor, Scott Wolven; my generous instructors from The Writer's Center in Bethesda, Maryland: Judith Harris, Meg Eden, Nan Fry, Claudia Gary; and from *Sun Magazine's* annual conference, "Into the Fire": Heather Sellers, Sy Safransky, and Sparrow

and with special gratitude for the artistry and support of Christine Cote at Shanti Arts

ABOUT THE AUTHOR

photograph: Sonya Melescu

Lee Woodman is the winner of the 2020 William Meredith Prize for Poetry. Her essays and poems have been published in *Tiferet Journal, Zócalo Public Square, Grey Sparrow Press, The Ekphrastic Review, vox poetica, The New Guard Review, The Concord Monitor, The Hill Rag, Naugatuck River Review,* and *The Broadkill Review.* A Pushcart nominee, she received an Individual Poetry Fellowship from the DC Commission on the Arts and Humanities in 2019 and 2020. Her poetry collections *Mindscapes,* published by Poets' Choice Publishing, and *Homescapes,* published by Finishing Line Press, came out in 2020. *Lifescapes* was published by Kelsay Books in summer 2021.

Woodman's radio and film awards include five CINEs, two NY International Film Blue Ribbons, and three Gracies from American Women in Radio and Television. She worked for twenty years in leadership roles at the Smithsonian Institution and was Vice-President of Media and Editorial at K12, Inc. As Executive Producer at Lee Woodman Media, Inc., her clients included The Library of Congress, The World Bank, Public Radio International, NPR, and the Fulbright Program. She has a bachelor's degree in art from Colby College and a master's degree in art education from Hartford Art School.

Shanti Arts

Nature • Art • Spirit

Please visit us online
to browse our entire book catalog,
including poetry collections and fiction,
books on travel, nature, healing, art,
photography, and more.

Also take a look at our highly
regarded art and literary journal,
Still Point Arts Quarterly, which
may be downloaded for free.

www.shantiarts.com

CPSIA information can be obtained
at www.ICGtesting.com
Printed in the USA
FSHW020113070122